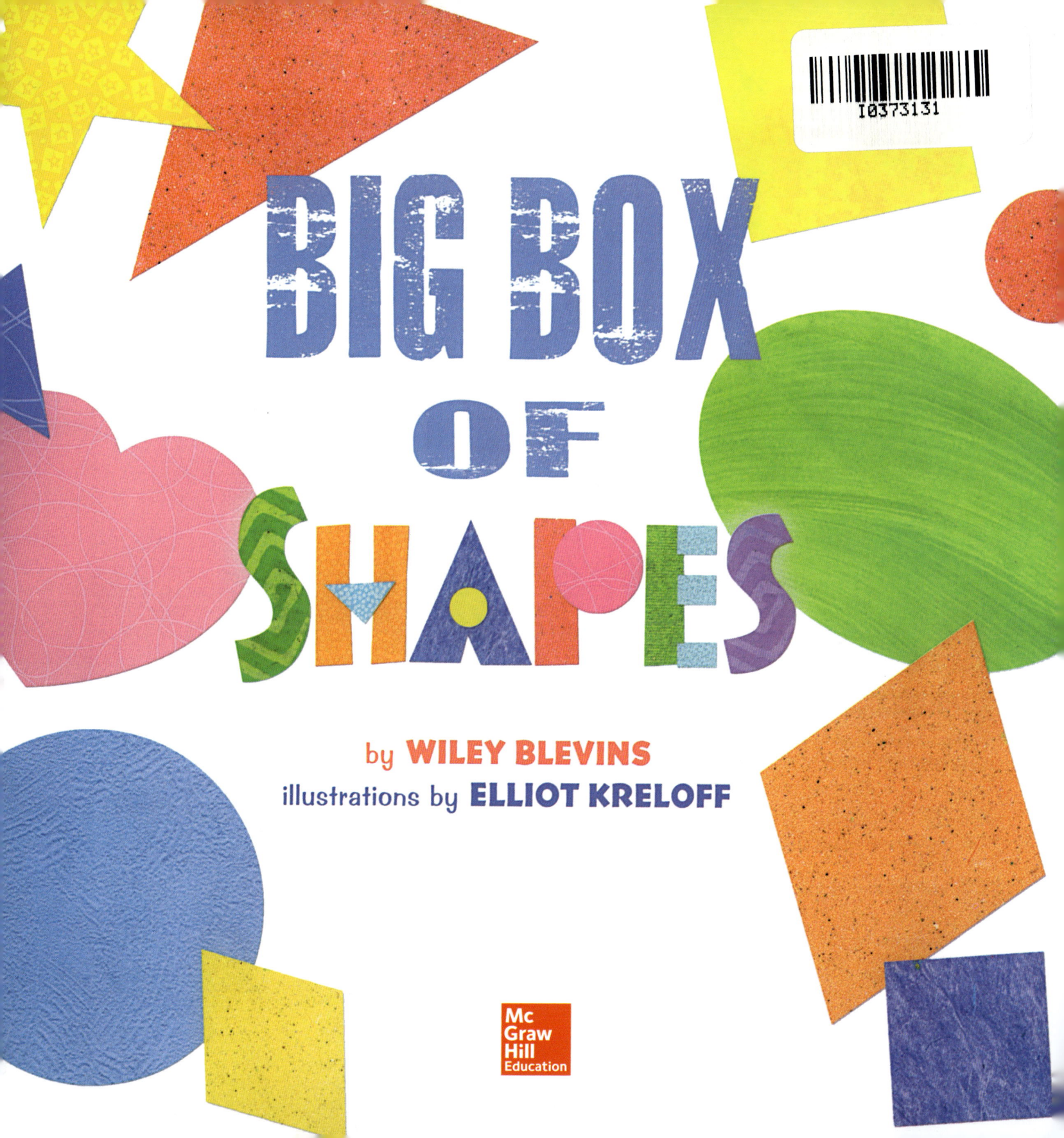

mhreadingwonders.com

©2016 Red Chair Press LLC.
All rights reserved.
Used with permission.

No part of this publication may be reproduced
or distributed in any form or by an means,
or stored in a database or retrieval system, without the
prior written consent of McGraw-Hill Education,
including, but not limited to, network storage or
transmission, or broadcast for distance learning.

Send all inquiries to:
McGraw-Hill Education
Two Penn Plaza
New York NY 10121

ISBN: 978-0-07-678747-0
MHID: 0-07-678747-8

Printed in China

7 8 9 10 11 DSS 28 27 26 25 24

Lulu and Max found a box.
It was filled with many shapes.

Lulu pulled out a square.

Then she took out a triangle.
"I'll put it on top," she said.
What did Lulu make?

A house.

"I will live in the house with my grandma and grandpa," said Lulu.

Max took a big circle from the box.

Then he added three smaller circles.
"Now it needs a smile," said Max.
What did Max make?

A happy face.

"That makes me smile, too" said Lulu.

"Look," yelled Lulu. "A rectangle." She added two small circles and a square to it.

What did Lulu make now?

A truck. Vroom. Vroom.

Lulu shared her shapes with Max.
"Thank you," said Max.
"I will use them to make a
hat for my happy face."

Lulu and Max dug deeper into the box.
They found more shapes.

Lulu made a kite with a diamond and a magic wand with a star.

Max made a turtle with an oval...

and sunglasses with two hearts.

"There are so many shapes in here," said Lulu and Max.
"Hmmm. What else can we make?"

Lulu and Max stacked the shapes up, up, up.
And what did they make?

A BIG MESS!